AMAZING PLANTS

By Honor Head

Gareth Stevens
Publishing

Please visit our web site at www.garethstevens.com.
For a free catalog describing our list of high-quality books, call 1-800-542-2595 (USA) or 1-800-387-3178 (Canada). Our fax: 1-877-542-2596

Library of Congress Cataloging-in-Publication Data
Head, Honor.
      Amazing plants / Honor Head.
         p. cm. — (Amazing life cycles)
      Includes index.
      ISBN-13: 978-0-8368-8897-3 (lib. bdg.)
      ISBN-10: 0-8368-8897-9 (lib. bdg.)
      1. Plants—Juvenile literature.   2. Plant life cycles—Juvenile
literature.   I. Title.
      QK49.H423   2008
      580—dc22   2007043114

This North American edition first published in 2008 by
Gareth Stevens Publishing
A Weekly Reader® Company
1 Reader's Digest Road
Pleasantville, NY 10570-7000 USA

This U.S. edition copyright © 2008 by Gareth Stevens, Inc. Original edition copyright © 2007 by ticktock Media Ltd.
First published in Great Britain in 2007 by ticktock Media Ltd., Unit 2, Orchard Business Centre, North Farm Road,
Tunbridge Wells, Kent, TN2 3XF United Kingdom

ticktock Project Editor: Ruth Owen
ticktock Project Designer: Sara Greasley
With thanks to: Sally Morgan and Elizabeth Wiggans

Gareth Stevens Senior Editor: Brian Fitzgerald
Gareth Stevens Creative Director: Lisa Donovan
Gareth Stevens Graphic Designer: Alex Davis
With thanks to: Mark Sachner

Photo credits (t = top; b = bottom; c = center; l = left; r = right):
Arcticphoto.co.uk: 9c. Corbis: 27. FLPA: 12b, 13, 16b, 17t, 18c, 19t, 26b, 28b, 30b, 31t. Floridanature.com: 28tl, 29t.
Nature Picture Library: 19 main. Shutterstock: cover, title page, contents page, 4tl, 4c, 4b, 5tl, 5r, 5cl, 5bl, 6tl, 6l, 6r,
7cr, 7 main, 8tl, 9t, 9b, 10tl, 10 main, 11t, 11b, 12tl, 12tr, 12cr, 14–15 all, 18tl, 18b, 20tl, 22tl, 22–23 all, 25bl, 25br, 26tl,
30tl. Stephen Mifsud – www.MaltaWildPlants.com: 24tl, 24b, 25t. Superstock: 7t, 16tl, 17b, 20l, 21tr, 21 main, 26c,
29b, 31b. ticktock image archive: map page 8.

Every effort has been made to trace copyright holders, and we apologize in advance for any omissions. We would be pleased to insert the appropriate acknowledgments in any subsequent edition of this publication.

Printed in the United States of America

1 2 3 4 5 6 7 8 9 10 09 08 07

Contents

Words in the glossary appear in **bold type** the first time they are used in the text.

What Is a Plant?

We eat the fruits of an orange tree.

Plants are living things that grow out of the ground. Most plants produce flowers, **fruits**, and **seeds**. Plants come in many different shapes and sizes. Trees and shrubs are also plants.

Most plants produce flowers. The flowers are often brightly colored.

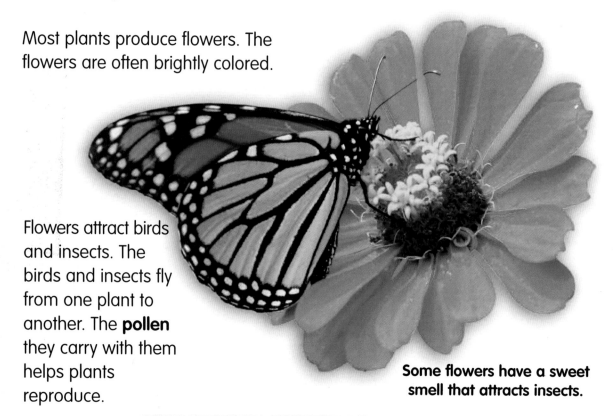

Flowers attract birds and insects. The birds and insects fly from one plant to another. The **pollen** they carry with them helps plants reproduce.

Some flowers have a sweet smell that attracts insects.

Grass is a plant that many animals eat.

Wheat is one type of plant. We call its seeds grain. We cannot eat grains raw, but we make them into flour and use them to make bread.

AMAZING PLANT FACT
A tree is a plant. Some trees can live for thousands of years.

Ferns

Mosses and ferns are plants that do not produce flowers.

Mosses and ferns grow in damp places that don't get much light. **Moss**

Parts of a Plant

The bird-of-paradise plant has a flower that looks like a bird!

Plants have roots, stems, and leaves. Most plants have roots that grow in the ground. The roots push down into the soil to hold the plant in place. The stem, leaves, and flowers are above the ground.

Plants make their own food. The plant's leaves use air and sunlight to make food. This process is called **photosynthesis**.

The plant's stem carries **nutrients** from the roots to the other parts of the plant. The stem also pushes the leaves upward toward sunlight.

The plant's roots suck up water and nutrients from the soil to feed the plant.

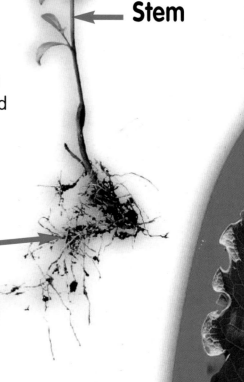

Leaves

Stem

Roots

The stems of some plants grow around other plants. Lianas have stems that wrap around tree trunks.

Tree trunk

Liana stem

A tree trunk is actually a hard, woody stem.

Living stone

Living stones are odd-looking plants that grow among rocks and pebbles. They have two thick leaves that look like stones on the ground.

The parts of a plant come in many shapes, sizes, and colors.

Plant Habitats

Saguaro (suh-WAHR-oh) cactuses grow in dry areas of the Southwest.

A **habitat** is the place where a plant or an animal lives. Plants can grow in many habitats—even under the sea! The greatest number of different plants grow in warm, wet tropical rain forests.

Plants live in every major habitat in the world.

Habitats Map

Map Key

Temperate grasslands: areas that are dry in summer	
Tropical grasslands: hot, dry areas with few trees	
Water	
Tundra: cold, windy places	
Temperate forests	
Arctic/Antarctica: frozen, snowy ground and icy seas	
Cold forests	
Warm, wet rain forests	
Deserts: dry land with little rain	
Mountains	

Long strands of seaweed grow in the ocean. Seaweed is a plant without roots. It has a special part called a holdfast to keep it in one place.

Seaweed uses its holdfast to cling to rocks.

On the icy Arctic tundra, plants grow close to the ground in clumps to avoid the cold wind.

AMAZING PLANT FACT

The sharp spines on a cactus are actually the plant's leaves. The spines lose less water than normal leaves in the hot desert.

Some Arctic plants have hairs on their leaves, stems, and buds for protection.

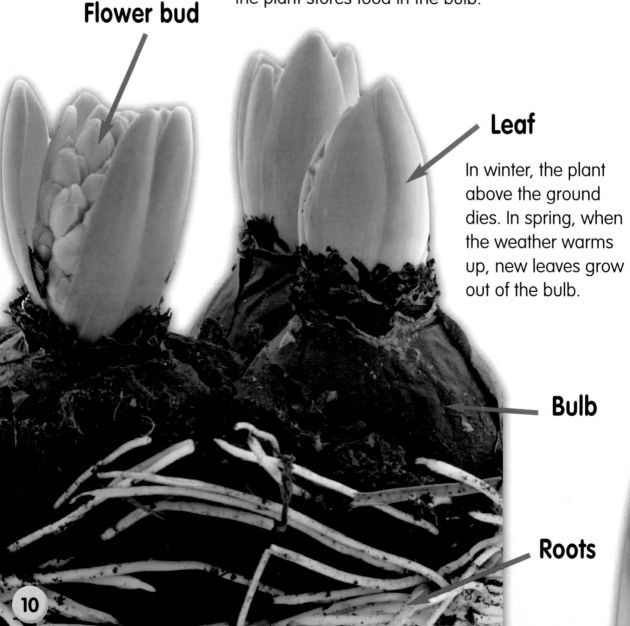

The black dots in a kiwifruit are its seeds.

Seeds and Bulbs

New plants can grow from a seed or a bulb. A seed is like a small case that contains everything needed to make a new plant.

A bulb grows underground, at the bottom of the plant. During summer, the plant stores food in the bulb.

Flower bud

Leaf

In winter, the plant above the ground dies. In spring, when the weather warms up, new leaves grow out of the bulb.

Bulb

Roots

Stigma

Most plants have flowers. The male parts, called stamens, are in the middle of the flower. Each stamen has an anther at the top.

The flower's anthers are covered in a fine yellow dust called pollen. The female part is called the carpel. It has a section called a stigma at the top.

Anther

Bees and other insects carry pollen from the anthers of one flower to the stigma of another flower. This is called **pollination**. After pollination, a seed is made.

AMAZING PLANT FACT

Bees visit flowers to collect sweet **nectar**. Bees use nectar to make honey.

This bee is covered with pollen from the anthers of a flower.

Scattering Seeds

Nature has many ways of carrying seeds from plants to grow in new places. Some seeds float away from their mother plant on water. Others are carried by animals or blown away by the wind.

Wind blows dandelion seeds to a new place to live.

Tumbleweed is a bush that breaks away from its roots in the autumn. The wind pushes it along the ground, and it scatters its seeds as it rolls along.

Tumbleweed

Some animals spread seeds. Squirrels collect and bury acorns. The acorns they don't eat may one day grow into oak trees.

Acorns are fruit from oak trees. Their hard shell protects the seeds inside.

This macaw is eating a palm fruit.

AMAZING PLANT FACT

When birds eat fruit, the seeds pass through the birds and fall to the ground in their droppings. The seeds grow into new plants.

Sunflower seeds are a tasty snack for birds and people.

What Is a Life Cycle?

A **life cycle** is the different stages that a plant or an animal goes through in its life. This diagram shows the usual life cycle of most plants.

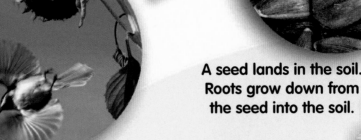

1

A seed lands in the soil. Roots grow down from the seed into the soil.

THE LIFE CYCLE OF A SUNFLOWER

8

The seeds fall to the ground. Birds eat the seeds and spread them in their droppings.

Insects pollinate the flower.

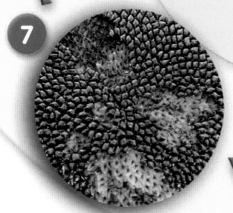

7

6

The plant makes new seeds.

Amazing Plant Life Cycles

Pitcher plant

In the pages that follow, we will learn about the life cycles of some amazing plants—from meat-eating pitcher plants to coconut palm trees.

Coconut palm tree

2

A stem grows upward from the seed and pushes through the soil.

3

Tiny leaves appear on the stem.

4

A bud appears and grows into a flower.

5

The stem grows taller and stronger. More leaves grow. The leaves get bigger.

The bud of a rafflesia
flower looks like a
large cabbage.

Rafflesia

The rafflesia is the world's biggest flower. It grows to nearly 3 feet (1 meter) across and can weigh more than 20 pounds (9 kilograms). This strange plant has no stem, leaves, or roots.

AMAZING PLANT FACT

The rafflesia is a rare sight. Its flower takes months to develop and lives for only a few days.

Many plants have colorful flowers and a strong smell to attract insects. The rafflesia flower appears when the plant is ready to be pollinated.

Most people think the rafflesia has a terrible smell. It smells like rotten eggs. Flies love the smell, however, and are attracted to the flower.

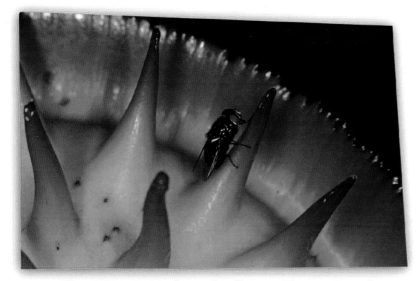

Flies take nectar from the flower. The center of a rafflesia flower holds several gallons of nectar.

The flies crawl around the rafflesia and get covered with pollen. They then spread the pollen from one flower to others.

The rafflesia grows in rain forest habitats in Southeast Asia.

Pitcher plants come
in many shapes
and colors.

Pitcher Plant

Pitcher plants grow in rain forests and other places where the ground is damp. Pitcher plants are **carnivores**, or meat eaters. They have a special bowl, or pitcher, that traps insects and other **prey**.

Ant

The pitcher is like a thin tube. When an insect comes to taste the nectar inside the tube, it slides down the slippery sides. It cannot escape.

The insect drowns in the pool of juice at the bottom of the tube. Its body is broken down and digested by the plant.

**AMAZING
PLANT FACT**
Some pitcher plants can
eat snails, frogs, and
even small mice!

The pitcher plant grows flowers in early spring. Bees pollinate the flowers.

After pollination, the plant makes seeds inside the flowers. The seeds fall to the ground when they are ready to grow.

Flower

The pitcher is part of the leaf.

Leaf

Tendril

The pitcher is attached to the leaf by a long, thin tendril.

The saguaro cactus can be 50 feet (15 m) tall.

Saguaro Cactus

The saguaro cactus can live for more than 100 years. The saguaro begins to produce flowers when it is about 35 years old.

In spring, buds appear on top of the main trunk and arms. The buds open into large white flowers.

Bats, bees, and birds feed on nectar from the flowers. They pick up pollen from the flowers on their bodies.

AMAZING PLANT FACT

Saguaro flowers open in the middle of the night. They close up again during the heat of the day.

The plant's sharp spines keep animals from eating it.

Animals carry pollen from one cactus to another. This allows pollination to occur, and the cactus produces seeds. One saguaro produces tens of thousands of seeds each year.

Gila woodpeckers make nest holes in a saguaro's trunk.

The Gila woodpecker carries pollen from one saguaro to another.

Flower

Bud

Coconut Palm Tree

Coconut palm trees have both male and female flowers. After the tree has flowered, it makes new seeds. The fruits of a palm tree are called coconuts.

Inside a coconut is the white part, called meat, which we can eat.

AMAZING PLANT FACT
Coconut shells can be used to make pots and cups.

Coconuts grow in bunches under the palm tree's leaves.

When the coconuts are ripe, they fall to the ground.

Young coconuts are filled with a sweet liquid that people can drink.

Coconut palms often grow on beaches. Many coconuts are washed out to sea. They float along until they land on another beach.

When the coconut reaches a new place, shoots start to grow out of it. These shoots grow into a new palm tree. The tree will be ready to flower and produce seeds in about seven years.

Shoot

Eye

Inside the skin of a coconut is a hard, hairy shell that protects the seeds. The shell has three "eyes." The new shoots grow from the eyes.

The plant's yellow flowers
are pollinated by bees
and other insects.

Fruit

Squirting Cucumber

The squirting cucumber grows on sandy
or stony ground. The plant has a thick,
hairy stem that trails along the ground.
The fruit of the plant is long and green.
It looks like a small, hairy cucumber.

The fruit fills up with juice and seeds.
It gets fatter and fatter. When the
fruit is ripe, it suddenly explodes!
The seeds inside shoot out.

**AMAZING
PLANT FACT**

The seeds of the squirting
cucumber shoot out of the
fruit at nearly 60 miles
(100 kilometers)
per hour!

Each fruit contains 25 to 50 seeds.

This fruit has dried up.
Some seeds are still stuck inside.

Seed

The squirting cucumber belongs to a group of plants called gourds. The fruits can be dried and the empty shells used to make cups, bowls, and musical instruments.

Gourds have fruits with a hard outer covering.

This is a gourd rattle.

Elephants eat fruit from
baobab trees.

Baobab Tree

Baobab trees live on hot grasslands in Africa, where it doesn't rain very often. When it does rain, the tree can store thousands of gallons of water in its thick trunk.

The baobab tree stays bare for nine months of the year. Then it grows leaves and flowers. The big white flowers open during the night.

The flowers' sweet smell attracts **nocturnal** animals, such as bats. These animals are active at night. The animals carry pollen to other flowers and help pollinate them.

The tree produces big fruits. Animals that eat baobab fruit spread seeds in their droppings.

Baobab flowers have a sweet smell.

The fruit of a baobab tree is called monkey bread. It holds many seeds.

It is easy to see why the baobab is also called the upside down tree. It looks as if its roots are growing at the top of the tree.

AMAZING PLANT FACT

A baobab tree starts flowering when it is about 20 years old. It can live for more than 1,000 years!

The leaves of ferns
are called fronds.

Resurrection Fern

This fern lives by attaching itself to another plant. It lives on large trees, such as oak trees. The fern gets the water and nutrients it needs from the **bark** of the tree and from the air.

When there is no rain, the fronds of the resurrection fern turn brown, shrivel up, and look dead. The fern can live like this for years.

AMAZING PLANT FACT

The word *resurrection* means "to come back to life." This fern gets its name because it appears to be dead but comes back to life!

After just one rain shower, the fronds uncurl, turn green, and seem to come back to life.

Ferns do not make seeds. Instead they have tiny **spores**. The spores are so small that we need a microscope to see them.

Spores grow on the underside of fronds.

These brown spots are called sori. The spores are inside the sori.

Spores are carried by wind. When a spore lands in a new place, it grows a thin root called a rhizoid. This root supplies the spore with water. The spore grows into a new fern.

The fruit of a corn plant is a favorite food of humans and animals.

That's Amazing!

Plants are a very important part of every habitat. Plants release **oxygen**, which we need to breathe. Plants also give animals and people food and shelter. In return, animals help plants survive in many ways!

This ant is feeding on the spores of a fern. Ants live in the fern's stem. They drag leaves and other pieces of dead plant material back to their nest. This makes **compost**, which is filled with nutrients. The fern then feeds on the compost.

Ant

The spores are inside the orange sori.

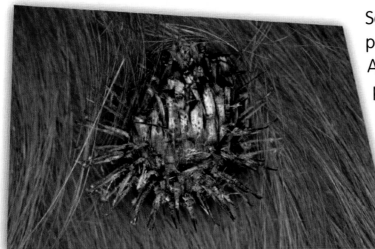

Sometimes animals brush past plants that have **burrs**. A burr is a seed with a prickly covering. The burrs get stuck in the animals' hair or fur. The animals carry the burrs to a new place where the seeds can grow.

A burr from a burdock plant has attached itself to an animal's fur.

Some plants have flowers that look like insects or birds. This tricks insects and birds into visiting the plant and pollinating it.

AMAZING PLANT FACT

The bee orchid has a flower that looks like a bee. These flowers attract real bees, which pollinate them.

Glossary

bark: the outer layer of a tree's trunk

burrs: seeds with a prickly covering

carnivores: animals or plants that eat meat

compost: dead leaves and pieces of plants that have mixed with soil and that provide nutrients for plants

fruits: fleshy parts of a plant that contain the plant's seeds

habitat: the natural conditions in which a plant or an animal lives

life cycle: the series of changes that a plant or an animal goes through in its life

nectar: a sweet liquid inside flowers. Insects and birds drink nectar.

nocturnal: active at night

nutrients: substances that nourish animals and plants

oxygen: a gas that all animals need to stay alive

photosynthesis: the process in which plants make their food

pollen: a fine dust produced by plants that helps them make seeds

pollination: the transfer of pollen from the male parts of a flower to the female parts of a flower

prey: animals that are eaten by plants or other animals

seeds: small parts of a plant that are the first stage of the plant's life

spores: the first stage of life for plants that do not produce seeds

Index

la ropa y cocinar. Las lámparas se tallaban de piedras blandas y se llenaban con aceite de grasa de ballena y una mecha de musgo seco.

Lemming En el Ártico hay muchos de estos animales parecidos a los ratones. Viven en túneles bajo la tierra y la nieve, donde hace mucho más calor que en la superficie. En invierno su piel cambia de color café a blanco: es el único roedor cuya piel cambia de color.

Lobo Los lobos cazan en manadas obedeciendo a un líder. Forman familias muy unidas, y los adultos son tiernos y juguetones con sus crías.

Manoplas Si un inuk necesita descansar y no tiene refugio, se saca las manoplas y se sienta encima de ellas.

Máscaras Los inuit creían que los curanderos podían hablar con los espíritus. Los curanderos cambiaban de máscaras para llevar a cabo las diferentes ceremonias. Los artistas inuit todavía hacen máscaras, pero por lo general son para decoración y no para uso ceremonial.

Morsa Estos mamíferos viven en banquisas de hielo (capas de hielo de varios pies de grueso y varias millas de extensión) que flotan sobre el océano Ártico. Para alimentarse, rastrean con sus bigotes el fondo del mar en busca de comida. Con sus colmillos guían a sus crías, rompen el hielo y pelean. Su nombre científico, *odobenidae*, quiere decir "aquellos que caminan con los dientes". Los inuit usan la piel de morsa para hacer hilo de pescar y embarcaciones, y su carne como alimento.

Oso polar Estos osos son los más grandes del mundo. Viven en islas de hielo en el extremo norte de la región, donde se confunden con el paisaje blanco. Su nombre inuit es "nanook". El oso polar es el animal más peligroso del Ártico.

Parka Esta típica chaqueta con gorro se usó por primera vez en el Ártico. Las parkas de las mujeres tienen un bolsillo extra en la espalda para llevar a los niños.

Perdiz blanca Estos pájaros se encuentran en toda Alaska. Son de color blanco-nieve en el invierno y tienen plumas en las patas para protegerse del frío. Ponen un huevo cada siete días, y éste es un alimento muy apreciado por los inuit. Existen otras dos variedades de perdiz: la perdiz de piedra y la coliblanca. La perdiz blanca es el pájaro oficial del estado de Alaska.

Perro Tradicionalmente los inuit se desplazaban en trineos tirados por perros. Hoy en día, muchos inuit también viajan por la nieve en vehículos motorizados.

Salmón Se puede encontrar una gran variedad de salmón en los ríos y arroyos de Alaska. Los inuit pescan salmones en verano. Para tener alimento durante el invierno, los ahúman, los secan o los guardan en el permafrost, la capa de tierra que está justo debajo de la superficie y que permanece congelada todo el año.

Umiak Estos botes están hechos de huesos de ballena cubiertos por pieles de animales. Se usan como medio de transporte y para cazar ballenas. El kayak es una versión más pequeña, más común y más conocida de este bote.